D1458463

The

Wit & Wisdom

of

NANI A.
PALKHIVALA

The

Wit &
Wisdom

of

NANI A.
PALKHIVALA

Compiled by JIGNESH R. SHAH

RUPA

Published by
Rupa Publications India Pvt. Ltd 2015
7/16, Ansari Road, Daryaganj
New Delhi 110002

Sales Centres:

Allahabad Bengaluru Chennai
Hyderabad Jaipur Kathmandu
Kolkata Mumbai

ISBN: 978-81-291-3747-0

Second impression 2015

10 9 8 7 6 5 4 3 2

The moral right of the author has been asserted.

Printed by Parksons Graphics Pvt. Ltd, Mumbai

Contents

Foreword

During his working life of over sixty years, my brother, the late Nani A. Palkhivala, gave unsparingly of himself and his thoughts to the country and the people, mainly through his writings and speeches. I have carefully preserved a sizeable portion of his articles, speeches and interviews to the media, and numerous write-ups on him in which he was quoted.

I had long been thinking of collating select quotations from his works so that his evocative words, pithy expressions and enlightened views may reach the younger generation and also be preserved for posterity. While I was in active practice, time was the constraint for me; after retirement, energy was the constraint. The project therefore remained in my heart but could not see the light of the day.

It came to fruition when one day I talked about it to Jignesh R. Shah, a practising lawyer and himself a writer of repute. He readily and enthusiastically took over the project and completed it with commendable accuracy and devotion.

The best of Nani, which is collected in this book for the future generations, is brought to the readers in the most presentable format, and will perpetuate Nani's memory as few other things can. It is a way of reaching out to a new generation of youth, many of whom have probably not come in contact with Nani. These youth are looking for direction and guidance in a world that has few icons of moral rectitude. Whilst most of them may not have the inclination and attention span to sit through Nani's books in their entirety, they are, as a generation, enthused by quotations. This book will serve the purpose of crystallizing Nani's wisdom in nuggets of beautifully written, yet easily accessible, prose. Here, Nani's witty and scintillating sentences have been carefully extracted from his works which would bring out in a nutshell—like a multi-vitamin capsule—the essence of his thoughts. It is this brevity and essence which distinguish this book from the existing literature of and about Nani. It will help the coming generation to understand the essence of what Nani stood for, and the reasons why he lives in our hearts today. And the Nani A. Palkhivala Memorial Trust is in the best position to publish this book of quotations, since it deals with the works of a man who was an equal master of both the spoken and the written word.

I am sure Nani's wit and wisdom contained in this book will serve to be a great source of inspiration to the people of India.

Mumbai   Behram A. Palkhivala

Preface

Nani Ardeshir Palkhivala (16 January 1920–11 December 2002) was a multitalented personality who played diverse roles in his rich life—lawyer, corporate director, diplomat, author, orator, political and economic thinker, and social reformer. His intellectual integrity, professional excellence and impeccable moral values made him a role model for an entire generation of Indians. A champion of civil liberties, he single-handedly defended the Constitution—and the citizens' rights under it—from the ill-intended amendments by the governments of the 1970s and 1980s, which aimed to give unlimited power to Parliament to alter the basic structure of the Constitution. He was one of the most influential intellectuals of his time who gave generously of his thoughts and his services to his country and countrymen. A brilliant orator, he became very popular even among common people with his annual budget speeches, delivered all over the country, in which he fearlessly tore apart the unprogressive economic policies and tyrannical taxation policies of the governments at the helm for over three decades. His contribution will be remembered for all time to come by the people of this country. But success and popularity did not change his character. He retained his innate humility, humanity and generosity all through his life. He was a philanthropist, and his spirituality transcended religious boundaries.

Many books have been written by him and about him, including a biography. This book contains select quotations—classified subject-wise under various chapters—from his writings and speeches over six decades of his working life. It has been brought out for those who did not have the advantage of hearing him. It is an effort to introduce him and his thoughts on a variety of subjects to a new generation. The book contains the distilled essence of Nani Palkhivala's wit and wisdom, the concise nature of the book making it more accessible.

This book originated as an idea in the mind of Nani Palkhivala's younger brother Behram Palkhivala, who is almost ninety years old now. Behram Palkhivala, himself a renowned lawyer and writer, had preserved with meticulous care, in six large boxes, most of the writings and speeches of Nani Palkhivala—by way of convocation addresses, budget speeches, interviews to the press, the chairman's statements (he was the chairman of ACC Ltd. for twenty-five years) and his other public lectures and articles in various newspapers and journals, such as *The Times of India*, *Indian Express*, *Hindustan Times*, *The Illustrated Weekly of India*, *The Economic Times*, *Sunday Standard*, *Janmabhoomi*, *Jam-e-Jamshed*, *Sanj Vartaman*, *Mid-Day*, *Afternoon*, *The Evening News*, *Himmat*, *India Today*, *Bhavan's Journal* and booklets published by the Forum of Free Enterprise.

Due to his advancing age and depleting energy, Behram Palkhivala felt he would not be able to undertake this book on his own. He therefore suggested that I take over the compilation of the book. He had, however, marked various quotations in the text of each article and speech which seemed worthy of being included. I picked up the boxes from his home and prepared the manuscript. We had long sessions at his home—discussing and debating which quotations to include and which to omit, and under which head or chapter, and in which sequence, the quotations should go. I prepared several drafts of the manuscript, and we went through many rounds of painstaking proofreading. For me, this journey of about a year with Behram Palkhivala was immensely educative and enriching—not only on the various subjects this book deals with, but also on the English language, grammar, punctuation, the art of writing, proofreading and, above all, on how to live life. Behram Palkhivala is a noble soul completely devoted to spirituality. He is humility personified and has always shunned publicity of any kind. He therefore did not allow his name to be credited as the author of this book. During the preparation of this book, I was amazed at the sharpness of his mind and his desire for excellence even at this age. He could quickly locate the minutest spelling errors, though his eyes could not bear the strain of reading. It would not be an exaggeration to state that this book is more his than it is mine. I have only been an instrument in fulfilling his long-cherished desire of bringing out this book. For conferring upon me the honour of being associated with this book and for showering his affection on me, I shall forever remain indebted to him.

I sincerely thank Mrs Rashmi Jehangir Palkhivala for her creative suggestions and the Nani A. Palkhivala Memorial Trust for their support in getting this book published.

In the end, I fervently hope that this book will

serve to be a great source of inspiration to the youth of this country.

Mumbai

16 January 2015

Jignesh R. Shah

Advocate, High Court

Introduction

The Nani A. Palkhivala Memorial Trust owes an immense debt of gratitude to Mr Behram Palkhivala and Mr Jignesh Shah for compiling, for publication, this immensely readable book containing quotations from Mr Nani Palkhivala's many writings and speeches.

The wide canvas on which Nani wrote and spoke constitutes a kaleidoscope which reflects his vast and varied interests, distinguished as much by the felicity of his language as by the profundity of his thoughts. To cull out from this vast body of collected wisdom the essential quotations, and systematically collate them in an easily accessible form could not have been an easy task. Mr Jignesh Shah, with Mr Behram Palkhivala's assistance, has done it admirably. For both of them it could only have been a labour of love.

For all those who espouse liberal thought and

cherish Nani's memory, this little book should be a source of inspiration and a constant companion.

Y.H. Malegam
Chairman
Nani A. Palkhivala Memorial Trust
Mumbai, 27 January 2015

I
Personalities

Men like Sri Aurobindo are examples of the mysterious reconciliation of incessant work and uninterrupted rest in one and the same person.

Three great passions dominated Sri Aurobindo's life: first, to liberate India from foreign rulers; second, to liberate India from Indians; and third, to liberate man from man.

No other thinker of modern times has tried so much, dared so much or seen so vividly the pattern of the human cycle down the ages and in the aeons of existence that lie ahead.

∞

Adi Sankara did not propound a religion, but propounded *the* religion which underlies all religions... He established the Empire of the Spirit.

The Jagadguru of Kanchi, Chandrasekharendra Saraswathi, personified the everlasting moral force. His was not a life to be described in words or measured in years. He lived in eternity.

∽

Dadaji Dilip Kumar Roy sang not only with his golden voice, but with every fibre of his being.

His art was a revelation, his voice got something of the music of the spheres and gave utterance to the eternal world itself.

∽

Mahatma Gandhi was the pilgrim of eternity—the man whose whole life was dedicated to endless seeking after endless truth.

He lit the imagination of the entire nation. He created men out of dust... He made heroes out of clay. Ordinary people became heroic... Women who would normally be afraid of a mouse would face bullets.

He took it upon himself to awaken the conscience of the human race. The world saw the astonishing phenomenon of a revolution led by a saint.

When Gandhiji smiled it was a public event; when he did not, it was a chapter of history.

On Gandhiji's visit to Panchgani: Winston Churchill was terribly clever, but he never understood one thing. He never understood how the presence of a toothless man in loin-cloth could translate a village into the capital.

∽

To question the enduring relevance of Sardar Vallabhbhai Patel to India today is like questioning the relevance of the sun to the solar system.

∽

C. Rajagopalachari: No problem was ever too big for his capacity or too small for his attention.

He had sometimes been wrong; but no other public figure had so often been right—and on so many diverse matters.

∽

On Dadabhai Naoroji's election to the House of Commons by a majority of three votes: There was a special virtue in the narrow majority; it relieved the voters of the effort to articulate the name Naoroji—they dubbed him 'Narrow-Majority'.

∽

Jayaprakash Narayan: Not since the time of Gandhiji

has moral force—personified by a frail individual—triumphed so spectacularly over the forces of evil. He changed decisively the course of history. One life transformed the destiny of hundreds of millions.

∽

Chief Justice M.C. Chagla: He wrote his judgments even as the grass grows—effortlessly, spontaneously. They are tinged with the essential characteristics of his own personality—sweetness and light.

His incredible open-mindedness has passed into a byword. No case was ever lost or won before him till the last word was spoken.

∽

Chief Justice J.C. Shah: In an age which applauded the vice of bias as the virtue of 'commitment', he was committed to nothing but right and justice.

There are no purple patches in his judgments. They are distinguished by logic and balance, precision and simplicity, not flowers or tears.

∽

Justice H.R. Khanna, on being denied by the government the post of chief justice for his judgment upholding the civil liberties of citizens: To the stature of such a judge, the chief justiceship of India could have added nothing.

∽

Chief Justice Meher Chand Mahajan: I never found him interrupt a good argument or endure the prolongation of a bad one.

∽

Justice Kuldip Singh: He has been known for his robust commonsense which has helped him to slice through legal intricacies and reach the core of the matter.

∽

Sir Jamshedji B. Kanga: A tall commanding figure, by his sheer presence he reduced all around him to less than life-size.

He had a mind that cut its way as instantly and easily to the very core of a problem as a hot knife through butter.

He had intellect enough to succeed without industry and industry enough to succeed without intellect.

∽

JRD Tata was essentially a realist. He believed in redeeming *Time*—the present moment. To him the Seven Wonders of the Modern World were Sunday, Monday, Tuesday, Wednesday, Thursday, Friday and

Saturday. He knew that the planes of Utopia and reality never coincide, and that the ideal cannot be institutionalized nor the institution idealized.

∽

Naoroji Godrej: His philanthropy, like Jamsetji Tata's, was constructively directed towards removal of the cause, and not the symptoms, of poverty and ignorance. Of him it could be truly said, 'He had an intelligent heart and a kind brain.'

∽

Sumant Moolgaokar of TELCO (now Tata Motors): To him perfection was a goal, never quite reached but always sought after.

He had an eye for the scarcest resource of all—talent; and he could bring out the best in his team. No one worked *under* him; everyone worked *with* him.

∽

Minoo Masani had an unsurpassed reputation as a man of total integrity in public life. And this quality by itself was sufficient to disqualify him from being a successful politician.

∽

Piloo Mody: Whereas some people take politics as a career, he sacrificed his career for the sake of politics.

∽

Nusserwanji P. Pavri, his school teacher: He brought the human touch into his lessons—it was always a lesson and never a lecture.

He read as if he were to live forever, even as he lived as if he were to die the next day.

By personal contact with him you not only learnt something, you became something.

∽

R.K. Laxman's cartoons: Laxman's creative genius scorches up what is false by a stroke as a flame. He depicts the trials and tribulations of the small man tossed about by politicians who plan for his future and refuse to face the reality that at the current rate of growth, India's time of economic 'arrival' will be 2100 A.D.

You see the March of Time—the forward-looking Common Man of 1947 turned into the disappointed man of 1952, battered in 1956 and shattered in 1963.

On India's Five Year Plans: The artist with vision sees what the purblind 'experts' miss—planning is excellent if you can plan and not make plans your master.

∽

2

Personal Reflections

My father taught me compassion and kindness for the less privileged... I welcomed anything from him, even if it was admonition, for I realized even then (as a small boy) what a noble and upright person he was and that he had ultimately my welfare in mind... He taught me rules of conduct which I have always tried to follow.

My mother was a woman of exceptionally strong character. She was an ideal mother—caring, gentle. In her quiet, unassuming way, she passed on many valuable lessons to me.

∞

To my parents, to their love and care and guidance, I owe a debt which could never be repaid. From them

I learnt that all the loveliness in the world can be reduced to its first syllable.

∽

I have deep faith in the existence of a force that works in the affairs of men and nations. You may call it chance or accident, destiny or god, Higher Intelligence or the Immanent Principle. Each will speak in his own tongue.

∽

Prayers have a higher purpose in life—what better way to come closer to our creator? I don't ask anything from god—if at all I do, it's to make me live a life according to Zarathushtra's will...I am content. Where is the place for more? My thanksgiving to Him would be in my being worthy of His kindness. If I could live the way He has asked us humans to, I would think of it as a way of repaying His kindness.

∽

At certain turning points in my life, when I would have made wrong decisions with my limited intelligence, I have felt as if my will was perceptibly bent by some higher power which saved me from myself.

∽

Frankly, I am not obsessed with material possessions or worldly success. I am far more attracted by things of the mind and the spirit.

∽

To me, money is only a means to an end. And that end is doing good to others.

∽

I can honestly claim that I am totally non-communal in my outlook and in all my private and public dealings. What matters most to me is the character and calibre of a person and not the religion which he practises.

∽

I take pains over whatever I say or write; and I am always dissatisfied with the quality of my speeches and my writings. It is this creative dissatisfaction which makes me try harder all the time.

∽

On the Zoroastrians having been given refuge and shelter in India:
If, in repaying the debt for the favour done to our ancestors more than 1300 years ago, I can play a tiny, even insignificant part, I shall regard my life as having been well spent.

∽

Life has taught me that when you have achieved everything that you have aimed for in life, you still feel something missing. To get what one wishes and to enjoy it too is seldom possible.

∽

My budget meeting will be considered successful only when that unknown little man who is interested in it comes to know of it and is enabled to attend it. Who knows, one day he may become the prime minister of India. (*'Sir, I used to listen to your speeches in Bangalore, and I respect you,'* Prime Minister H.D. Deve Gowda, *digressing from his prepared speech, told Nani at a book release function on 3rd January 1997.*)

∽

3
Philosophy of Life

There is an element of chance or destiny in everybody's life and only a fool refuses to recognize the presence of an 'undefinable force' that leads him.

❧

It is amazing how we learn through misfortune, and if you are sensitive you realize that nothing happens which does not contribute to the evolution of your spirit.

❧

There is more to life than success, and more to success than money. There is a spiritual side to man which alone can make him happy.

❧

You may not believe in a fate which overtakes men however they act; but you have to believe in a fate which overtakes men unless they act.

❧

Truth never yet fell dead in the streets—it has such great affinity with the soul of man.

❧

The law of karma postulates that in this world there are no rewards or punishments; it is simply a case of inevitable consequences. As you sow, so shall you reap. Sometimes others reap what you have sown.

❧

There is nothing like salvation on the cheap. There is no spiritual enrichment which money can buy. There are no fixed formulae, no rules of thumb, no prescriptions as in a pharmacopoeia.

❧

The path of the Spirit is narrow and there are yawning abysses on either side.

❧

Napoleon said: 'There are only two strong forces in the world; the sword and the spirit.' In the ultimate analysis the sword is always vanquished by the spirit. When you confront absolute power with absolute love, it is absolute love which triumphs.

∞

We are all insignificant members of an insignificant species on an insignificant planet in an infinite Universe.

∞

There is an interlinking and interconnection all around and at every level, in time and in space. No one lives, or possibly can live, in isolation. The past is linked to the future, this world to the next, men to their fellow-men, thoughts to actions, actions to reactions, the living spirits to the departed ones.

∞

Today, the world is gripped by a sickness—the mental sickness of the young as well as the old. Discotheques would not flourish, as they do, if young minds had something better to learn and something to understand. This mental sickness, the feeling of insecurity, of unhappiness amidst plenty, is the disease of affluence, which has afflicted men down the ages in all civilizations.

⚮

In the case of every soul, however troubled, restoration can come only from within. This is the lesson taught by the great Indian sages, from the nameless ones who lived in the twilight of history to Sri Aurobindo. It is the one lesson which we do not remember but which we can never wholly forget. There is still hope for India, and for the world, if we relearn this lesson today.

⚮

In these days of spiritual illiteracy and poverty of the spirit, when people find that wealth can only multiply itself and attain nothing, when people have to deceive their souls with counterfeits after having killed the poetry of life, it is necessary to remind ourselves that 'civilization is an act of the spirit'.

⚮

The beginning of obsolescence of materialistic civilization may not be far away. There are hopeful signs of a longing for that which a consumer culture cannot provide. A transformation is going on and it is probable that in our time we are going through the necessary travails before mankind ascends to a new awareness... During the transition, let us act in conformity with the words of buddhi—'We have not inherited this earth from our forefathers; we have borrowed it from our children'.

∽

4
Man

Man has been defined as a rational animal, but this definition was given to man by man himself in a characteristic moment of self-adulation.

∽

A great man is one in whose presence everybody feels great.

∽

A man is as small as the things that annoy him.

∽

Essentially human frailties and weaknesses are the same the world over. Man is the same trousered ape, whether he is in Delhi or in Detroit, whether he trudges barefoot on dusty roads or flies at 600 miles an hour.

❧

The explanation for our endless predicament is to be found in the basic fact that we are born of risen apes, and not of fallen angels. Our conflicts and crimes, our missiles and murders, should cause no surprise when we remember our predatory animal origin.

❧

The miracle of man is not how far he has sunk, but how magnificently he has risen. We are known among the stars by the *Mahabharata*, not by our riots and massacres.

❧

Though all of us belong to the same species of creation—*homo sapiens*—we are at different stages of evolution. Some men are closer to the brute from whom our species is believed to have evolved, and some to the supramental beings who will emerge after aeons of existence.

❧

There is a greater difference between man and man

than there is between some men and animals.

&

Nature has not read Article 14 of the Constitution which grants equality to all persons. Men are born unequal in character, in intelligence, in their capacity for hard work, their willingness to take risks, and their ability to take the initiative.

&

The modern man, despite all his comforts and conveniences, is still perplexed. He cannot call home the heart to quietness, because his spirit is not in tune with the infinite.

&

With our incredible scientific progress, we have reached a stage when the only threat to man, left to be met, is man himself.

&

Man is an unfinished creature. Past history bears witness to the fact that man is only a caricature of man to be. If a human being who lived 5000 years ago were to reappear in our midst, we would hardly recognize him as a member of our own species. Evolution is continuously progressing, and today's man will appear equally strange to the evolved human race 5000 years later.

∽

Humanity is in the making, and requires to be made.

∽

5
India—Ancient, Modern and Future

India is eternal, everlasting. Though the beginnings of her numerous civilizations go so far back in time that they are lost in the twilight of history, she has the gift of perpetual youth. Her culture is ageless and is as relevant to our twentieth century as it was to the twentieth century before Christ.

✍

This ancient civilization has survived and will survive when the raucous and fractious voices of today are lost in the silence of the centuries.

✍

Vedanta taught the technique of self-development. The ultimate destiny of man is to discover within himself the true self as the changeless behind the changing, the eternal behind the ephemeral, and the infinite behind the finite.

&

The *Upanishads* give us a glimpse of eternal truth on the wing, and they never need to be revised and updated. There is no comparison between the seers who wrote on the tablets of the heart and the scientist who wrote on paper yesterday what he has to erase today.

&

The rishis realized that each man has to work out his own salvation and that everyone's own spiritual experience is vital to the attainment of the ultimate state of the soul's evolution.

&

The rishis were fully aware of the ultimate reality which postulates that the boundary lines are superfluous, and the points of contact are real between the realms of the living and the non-living... Plants share the emotions of humans; and steel feels fatigue as much as animals. Harmony and unity—not dichotomy and divergence—is the ultimate reality.

&

The profound truth that all matter is nothing but energy seems to have been perceived by the rishis without the means of conducting any scientific experiments.

～

There is a unity underlying the entire creation. In the ultimate analysis there is no difference between mind and matter, between animate and inanimate creation. Shadow and sunlight, doubt and belief, microcosm and macrocosm, hardly seem to be opposites—as perceived by the seers, who had a unified vision of the Universe.

～

The vastest knowledge of today cannot transcend the buddhi of the rishis; and science, in its most advanced stage, is closer to Vedanta than ever before.

～

It would be restorative of national self-confidence to know that many discoveries of today are really re-discoveries and represent knowledge which ancient India had at her command.

～

'Civilization is an act of the spirit'. Ancient India was far more civilized than modern India with its satellites in space.

∽

Ancient India was great because it was as enamoured of learning as modern India is of petty politics.

∽

The soul of India aspires integration and assimilation. Over 5000 years, Indian civilization has been made richer and deeper as a result of absorbing what is best in outside influences and integrating them. This is what has made Indian culture such a living force of ineffable beauty.

∽

The contrast between the culture of ancient India and that of modern India seems sufficient to disprove Darwin's theory of evolution.

∽

It is the spirit of the nation that ultimately counts and, frankly, we have not recaptured the spirit that made us a great nation centuries ago.

∽

India is like a donkey carrying a sack of gold—the donkey does not know what it is carrying but is content to go along with the load on its back.

∽

When India became free, the first duty of the government should have been to see that our priceless heritage was made widely known and that young men and women were made to understand how fantastically rich our country is in its spiritual and intellectual treasures.

∽

Every nation gets obsolescent, even as a commercial product gets obsolescent, and the only way to prevent obsolescence of our nation is to hark back to our ancient heritage.

∽

There are two kinds of poverty—inward and outward. Outward poverty may be reduced by following economic policies. But inward poverty can be reduced only by reading our ancient literature.

∽

Our ancient heritage is a potent antidote to the current tendency to standardize souls and seek salvation in herds.

∞

After having unleashed the incredible power of the atom and the phenomenal forces of fission and fusion, we are back to the lesson taught in India 4000 years ago—that the greatest force in the world is love, and there has never been and will never be a substitute for it.

∞

This epoch of unbelief, however glittering, looks barren when compared to the glorious heritage of our country. People, especially in the West, feel dejected or lonely, as family bonds weaken. It is the great tradition of this ancient land which has kept people together—this tremendous cementing factor of family bonds will keep us together forever.

∞

Tall men dominated the scene, sixty years ago, in place of the pygmies who strut and fret their hour upon the stage today. After the passing away of those outstanding leaders, India became an orphan.

Our Constitution, which enjoins the unity and integrity of India, gave us a flying start; and equipped us adequately to meet the challenges of the future. Unfortunately, over the years, we dissipated every advantage we started with, like a compulsive gambler bent upon squandering an invaluable legacy.

∽

In the affairs of nations, as in the affairs of men, there is a providential margin of error: you may take wrong turns at the crossroads, misuse time, take gold for dross and dross for gold, and yet somehow stumble along to your destination. But the margin and period of permissible error need to be carefully watched. You overstep them at your peril.

∽

On the silver jubilee of India's independence: It may be a jubilee, but it is hardly an occasion for jubilance.

∽

The picture of India that emerges today is of a great nation in a state of moral decay, of which corruption and indiscipline are two of the several facets. In the land of Mahatma Gandhi, violence is on the throne today. Mobocracy has too often displaced democracy.

ల

India has undertaken, unilaterally and voluntarily, a project of moral disarmament.

ల

The tricolour fluttering all over the country is black, red and scarlet—black money, red tape and scarlet corruption.

ల

The greatest enemy of India today is not Pakistan or China, but Indians themselves. No enemy can possibly weaken the country so effectively as Indians can. The defences of our democracy may be impregnable from without, but they are vulnerable from within.

ల

It is not enough that we believe in our national motto, 'Truth will prevail'. Truth, no doubt, will ultimately prevail. But we must take active steps to ensure that falsehood does not have too long an innings before the ultimate moment of truth arrives.

ల

Like India, Israel is an old country but a young nation. We have a lot to learn from that country as to how democratic institutions should function, just as we have a lot to teach it, by our own sad example, how they ought not to function.

∽

We Indians are individually intelligent, but collectively foolish.

∽

In this ancient and unhurried civilization we seem to have no sense of time and no sense of urgency... In the national language, Hindi, the same word—kal—is used to denote both yesterday and tomorrow... Further, we believe in reincarnation. What does it matter if you waste this life? You will have many more lives in which to make good.

∽

We are content to fill the unforgiving year with sixty seconds' worth of distance run.

∽

The most persistent tendency in India has been to have too much government and too little administration; too many laws and too little justice; too many public servants and too little public service; too many controls and too little welfare.

∽

India has the gift of producing great souls in the darkest hour. I have a deep-seated faith that when the hour strikes, the man will be found.

∽

You must not forsake the ship because you cannot control the winds. Our motherland needs the services of our finest and most talented citizens.

∽

For Indians residing abroad to come back to India with their fortunes, is like entering into matrimony. It is easy to take the plunge but difficult to get out.

∽

A nation's worth is not measured merely by its gross national product, any more than an individual's worth is measured by his bank account... Even our poverty can be harnessed as a tremendous driving force in fulfilling great national purposes.

∽

Affluence has never been the yardstick for measuring the contribution of a nation to the growth and development of human civilization. Besides, in recorded history, nations and civilizations have perished through affluence; but no nation, no civilization, has died of adversity.

∞

The Indian's inner strength and capacity for patient endurance are almost unbelievable. The nation is able to take in its stride situations which would cause a revolution in other countries.

∞

We endure injustice and unfairness with feudalistic servility and fatalistic resignation.

∞

The trader's instinct is innate in Indian genes. An Indian can buy from a Jew and sell to a Scot, and yet make a profit!

∞

Fashions in ideas change, as do fashions in clothes. India is much less quick to follow new fashions in ideas than in dress.

∞

Among the nations of the world, India ranks very high in innate intelligence, but abysmally low in wisdom—what the ancient rishis called buddhi. This is both the cause and the effect of our total indifference towards education.

∽

History is replete with ironies. But it may be doubted whether the story of man affords a more tragic irony than the happenings in the Mahatma's motherland in the centenary year of his birth—the total disregard for his creed in economics and politics and the great schism within the Indian National Congress. Other countries have rejected their prophets; but only the daedal Indian mind can revere the Mahatma and reject his teachings.

∽

It is impossible to believe that this nation has lost its greatness forever. The time will come when it will redeem itself. After all, in our own times India represented the greatest moral force known to modern history and pushed back, without weapons, the largest empire on earth.

∽

I should like to reaffirm my unquenchable confidence in the long-term future of India. Our follies and misfortunes are not going to be forever. The oracle of today drops from his pedestal on the morrow. In the affairs of nations, as in the business of the elements, winds shift, tides ebb and flow, the boat rocks. Luckily, we have let the anchor hold. We have survived as a united democracy—a historic achievement.

∾

We shall reach out for the years ahead with assurance, sustained by the conviction that this country has a future far more glorious than its present. Let us have an unquenchable faith in the future and an unswerving confidence in our power to mould it.

∾

One day when the trivialities which engage our attention have died away, the spiritual truths which India has inherited will penetrate the mountains, cross the oceans and get known far and wide.

∾

The India of the future will find her identity only by going back to the India of the past.

∾

6

Constitution

Remember, the Constitution was meant to *constitute* the nation.

✑

The Constitution is intended not to provide merely for the exigencies of the moment but to endure through a long lapse of years. We should get accustomed to a spacious view of the great instrument.

✑

The Constitution was meant to impart such a momentum to the living principles of the rule of law that democracy and civil liberty may survive in India beyond our own times and in the days when our place will know us no more.

✑

The Constitution represents 'Charters of power granted by liberty', and not 'Charters of liberty granted by power'. Liberty is not the gift of the state to the people; it is the people enjoying liberty as the citizens of a free republic who have granted powers to the legislature and the executive.

∽

Our Constitution is not the cause, but a consequence, of personal and political freedom.

∽

We, the people of India, adopted, enacted and gave to ourselves the Constitution. We, the people, are also its only keepers.

∽

It is not the MPs, dressed in brief authority, who are supreme. It is the Constitution which is supreme. It is the eternal human freedoms which are supreme. It is the people who are supreme.

∽

It is not the Constitution which has failed the people, but it is our chosen representatives who have failed the Constitution.

In construing a Constitution what is implied is as much a part of the instrument as what is expressed, what is left unsaid is as important as what is said.

❧

The Constitution is not a jellyfish; it is a highly evolved organism. It has an identity and integrity of its own, the evocative Preamble being its identity card. It cannot be made to lose its identity in the process of amendment.

❧

The essential purpose of our Constitution is to ensure freedom of the individual and the dignity of man, and to put basic human rights above the reach of the state and of transient politicians in power whose naked juvenile chatter is covered by the fig leaf of demagogic claptrap.

❧

The Fundamental Rights are the very heart of our Constitution—taking them away would deprive the Constitution not only of its identity but of its life itself.

❧

What the Tenth Legion was to Julius Caesar, what the Old Guard was to Napoleon, what the Eighth Army was to Montgomery, the Fundamental Rights are to the citizen. Without them, it would be difficult, if not impossible, to guard the citadel of freedom.

∽

The protection of the citizen against all kinds of men in public affairs, none of whom can be trusted with unlimited power over others, lies not in their forbearance but in limitations on their power. At least such is the conviction underlying our Constitution.

∽

Citizens need protection against their own representatives, because men dazzled by the legitimacy of their ends seldom pause to consider the legitimacy of the means.

∽

While it is true that no one is above the law, it is equally true that, so long as our Constitution lasts, everyone is above state terrorism.

∽

The Directive Principles (in Part IV) are the *directory ends* of government, while the Fundamental Rights (in

Part III) are the *permissible means* for achieving those ends... An honest and competent government should be able to achieve the directory ends by the permissible means.

∽

There can be no conflict between the directory ends and the permissible means. The only conflict is between the Constitution and those who refuse to accept the discipline of the Constitution... No doubt, the discipline of human rights is irksome to those who think that all power is delightful and absolute power is absolutely delightful.

∽

The light went out of the Constitution when, in 1976, a few days after Diwali—the festival of lights—the Forty-Second Amendment was rushed through Parliament while most of the opposition leaders were languishing in jail without a trial. It is the light of the Constitution which has been rekindled by the Supreme Court (in the *Minerva Mills* case).

∽

The basic structure of the Constitution is of marble. Article 31C, as amended by section 4 of the

Forty Second Amendment Act, sought to substitute a framework of red bricks. The Supreme Court's judgment (in the *Minerva Mills* case) has cried a halt to the process of administering euthanasia to freedom.

☙

Article 31C (as amended in 1976) made the Constitution stand on its head. The Fundamental Rights which are enforceable were rendered unenforceable by Article 31C, while the Directive Principles which are unenforceable were virtually rendered enforceable against the citizen when they are pursued in violation of his Fundamental Rights.

☙

Article 368 which confers on Parliament the power to amend the Constitution cannot be read as expressing the death wish of the Constitution or as a provision for its legal suicide.

☙

In exercising its amending power, Parliament cannot arrogate to itself the role of the official liquidator of the Constitution.

☙

If Parliament had the power to destroy the basic structure of the Constitution, it would cease to be a creature of the Constitution and become its master.

∽

The donee of a limited power cannot, by the exercise of that very power, convert the limited power into an unlimited one. An organ established by the Constitution and vested with a limited amending power cannot make its own power unlimited while purporting to exercise that very power.

∽

Article 74 does not require the president to blindly accept the advice of the outgoing Council of Ministers to dissolve Parliament even if such advice is contrary to the spirit and intendment of the Constitution, e.g. when in times of political crisis it may result in frequent parliamentary dissolutions and fresh elections at short intervals: If the contrary view was correct, India could be engaged in two or three midterm polls every year, and the ballot box would become the national sport... To my mind it is an untenable proposition that in times of political instability every government going out of office by the revolving door is entitled to thrust parliamentary dissolution on the country as its parting gift and the president is bound to oblige meekly.

7
Education

Animals can be trained; only human beings can be educated.

∽

In a convocation speech addressing the fresh graduates as 'my fellow students': I call you fellow students because, I hope, I have not stopped learning.

∽

Education has been called the technique of transmitting civilization. In order that it may transmit civilization, it has to perform two major functions: it must enlighten the understanding and enrich the character.

The two marks of a truly educated man, whose understanding has been enlightened, is the capacity to think clearly and intellectual curiosity... If this habit of thinking for yourself has not yet been inculcated in you, you would be well advised to acquire it after you leave college... Intellectual curiosity would enable the student to continue, nay, to intensify, the process of learning after he has come out of the comfortable cocoon of the university and is thrown into the maelstrom of life.

(To enrich the character) what we need today more than anything else is moral leadership—founded on courage, intellectual integrity and a sense of values.

∽

In order to acquire education what is needed on the part of students is personal participation and transformation. Education cannot be given to anyone; it must be inwardly appropriated.

∽

You can lead a man to the university but you cannot make him think.

∽

Education is at the heart of the matter. Literacy is not enough. It is good to have a population which is able to read; but infinitely better to have people able to distinguish what is worth reading.

৵

Your education has been in vain if it has not fostered in you the habit of clear, independent thinking. There are well-dressed foolish ideas, just as there are well-dressed fools, and the discerning man must be able to recognize them as such.

৵

The aim of character-based higher education must be to leave you with a residuum called culture which would teach you a meaningful philosophy of life and enrich your character.

৵

Culture is what remains after you have forgotten all that you set out to learn.

৵

The first objective of higher education should be to turn out integrated personalities in whom have been inculcated noble ideals.

৵

Education is the rock on which India must build her political salvation. Our country will be built not on bricks but on brains; not on cement but on enlightenment.

❦

On the university campus we must stress the importance of individual self-fulfilment but not self-indulgence, group cohesiveness but not group jingoism, work and achievement but not power and acquisitiveness for their own sake.

❦

The child is father of the man. The quality of education of the children of today will determine the quality of life in India tomorrow.

❦

Value-based education is the only instrument for transmuting national talent into national progress.

❦

Knowledge can be intuitive and is not gained merely through sensory perception.

❦

We are quite right in making constant endeavours to raise the standard of living of our people. But the standard of life is even more important than the standard of living. If we lose our sensitivity towards the quality of life, it can only mean that while our knowledge increases, our ignorance does not diminish.

༄

Knowledge is the only instrument of production which is not subject to diminishing returns.

༄

When you educate a boy you educate an individual, but when you educate a girl you educate a whole family.

༄

History will record that the greatest mistake of the Indian republic in the first forty years of its existence was to give abysmally low priority to education—in fact no priority at all.

༄

The best charity which one can do in India today is to carry knowledge to the people.

༄

Unfortunately, in our own times, we have downgraded the intellectual and have in fact devalued the very word. Today an 'intellectual' means a man who is intelligent enough to know on which side his bread is buttered.

∽

At their best, some of our present-day universities are academic cafeterias offering junk food for the mind. At their worst, they are the breeding-grounds of corruption and indiscipline, dishonesty and irresponsibility.

∽

We continue to churn out ethical illiterates and moral idiots. Our education continues to be value-agnostic and value-neutral.

∽

Today the university student is aware that what he knows does not count in the examination half as much as who he knows.

∽

In the good old days college buildings did not leak— nor did the examination papers.

∽

8

Democracy and Freedom

I would define 'democracy' as the dwelling place which man has built for the spirit of liberty. Intruders have seized the place in many lands. A democracy in which the spirit of liberty does not reside is a morgue.

❧

Democracy and freedom are not synonymous. Adult franchise may merely amount to the right to choose your tyrants. In Lord Hailsham's words, you may have 'elective dictatorship'. Hence the conviction shared by several countries about the sovereign virtue of having a Bill of Rights in the Constitution which would guarantee basic human freedom.

❧

Let us make no mistake: civil liberty and individual freedom can die as surely, though not as swiftly, in a democracy as it can in a totalitarian state. The nose-counting method—one man, one vote—will certainly survive. But it is only the husk of democracy. When civil liberties and individual freedom are excessively restricted, it is poor consolation to know that the persons responsible for such a state of affairs were the elected representatives of the people.

∽

A law does not cease to be tyrannical because it has been passed by the elected representatives of the people.

∽

Democratically elected representatives of the people can act no less foolishly, and often no less oppressively, than authoritarian states.

∽

Freedom cannot be inherited in the bloodstream. Each generation will have to defend it and fight for it—then alone will it survive to be passed on to the next.

∽

Freedom is fragile. It is not hewn out of granite. Unless the people take interest in public affairs, the chances of freedom surviving are very slight.

✶

When we live in a democracy, we live in hazard. There is no amenable god in it, no particular concern or mercy. Democracy involves the cooperation of all perceptive citizens in the active work of running the country. It means payment to the state, not only in taxes but in time and in thought.

✶

The thirst for freedom can never be quenched in the human breast... But the 'one man, one vote' rite is not enough to make a democracy meaningful. Every democracy must have an aristocracy of talent, of knowledge and of character. It is this aristocracy which must take to public life, however distasteful it may be.

✶

Freedom is like hunger—just as one cannot eat for tomorrow, so one cannot be free today for tomorrow. The cost of food and freedom is an ongoing cost and every generation must continue to pay for it or run the risk of losing something precious.

∞

Adult franchise as practised in India is the worst possible advertisement for its true virtues.

∞

Justice Frankfurter observed that in a democracy the highest office is that of a citizen. All of us are born to that most important office, but few of us discharge the duties attached to that office. This is the root cause of most of our ills.

∞

There is no democracy for keeps, there is no democracy for all time to come. It is only to the extent to which the people are devoted to the cause of freedom that a democratic set-up has a chance of survival.

∞

Democracy is never a destination reached but always a beckoning goal calling upon every citizen to play his part in a dedicated spirit in the great endeavour of nation-building.

∞

Today the people of India associate democracy with guns, goons and gold. One of the most thoughtful remarks of de Tocqueville was that democracy throws mediocrity into power. But the situation becomes intolerable when democracy throws criminals into power.

∞

Decency in public life is the only solution if we are to preserve the true spirit of democracy and not be left merely with the husk of a comatose Constitution. We are faced with the stark alternatives of either dharma in public life or the twilight of Indian democracy.

∞

Since man does not know how to behave, the necessity arises of legal responsibilities to prevent liberty from degenerating into licence.

∞

Liberty has a hypnotizing sound; while, unfortunately, responsibility has no sex appeal.

∞

Liberty without accountability is the freedom of the fool... Our concept of freedom will remain an impoverished one until it is rounded and deepened by value-based education. Till then we shall continue to work as a third-class democracy under a first-class Constitution.

꙰

It is true that eternal vigilance is the price of liberty. But it is true, in even a deeper sense, that eternal responsibility is also part of the price of liberty. Excessive authority without liberty is intolerable; but excessive liberty without authority and without responsibility soon becomes equally intolerable.

꙰

When we became a republic, we forgot that freedom is like alcohol—it must be taken in moderation.

꙰

No virtue is absolute—not even freedom. One man's freedom fighter is another man's terrorist.

꙰

One of the consequences of the failure to educate our people is that we are oblivious of the need to combine freedom with order—order enforced by authority, and freedom exercised under authority.

Liberty is a virtue which can never stand alone but, as de Tocqueville said, it must be paired with a companion virtue: liberty and morality; liberty and law; liberty and justice; liberty and the common good; liberty and civic responsibility. The criminalization of politics and the deplorably low moral tone of our national life are the direct consequences of the failure to impart value-based education which would inculcate the need for the companion virtues which must be paired with liberty.

⚬

The right to dissent is at the heart of every democracy. This right becomes the duty of every knowledgeable and right-minded citizen, when government acts in a manner detrimental to civil liberties or otherwise against the public interest.

⚬

Never mistake the majority vote for a vote in favour of reason, for a vote in favour of what is right.

⚬

The greatest dangers to liberty lurk in encroachments on human rights by men whose purposes may be beneficent but who have no understanding of the damage they cause to human rights in the name of social justice.

∽

On elections after the Emergency: Our people demonstrated that liberty is not an 'optional extra' in a democracy, that human rights are not a luxury intended merely for the elite and the affluent, and that the poor can be as intensely committed to inalienable freedoms as the richest under the sun.

∽

Large republics and small hearts go ill together.

∽

Thought is certainly free in this country; what we lack is thought, not the freedom of thought.

∽

The greatest achievement of Indian democracy has been that it has survived unfractured for more than sixty years. The achievement is all the more creditable since no other democracy has had such diversity in unity and presents such a mosaic of humanity.

∽

Inflation devours democracy. It is the favourite food of that demon. No country which has suffered over 20 per cent inflation for long has ever survived as a democracy.

∽

There are three types of democracy. The first type of democracy is that which the Greeks knew, where the people acted according to their will, their whims, their fancies; and they did not like any restraints on their power to make any decision whatever by a majority vote. That was a primitive kind of democracy.

The second type is the democracy that our founding fathers brought into existence. It is the democracy where there is obedience to the law.

There is a third type of democracy where there is obedience to the unenforceable.

The first type of democracy is infantile. The second type of democracy I would call a teenager democracy. It has just attained majority, though not maturity; it is to be compared in intelligence and outlook to a person 18 years old. It will be a long time before the third type of democracy flourishes in India.

∽

Freedom is often assumed to be a basic tenet of life in a republic like ours and yet, in a sense, men are not born free. They are chained at the moment of birth by the umbilical cord and, even when that is severed, they remain navel-bound to the society into which they have been born.

∽

9

Socialism and Capitalism

True socialism means the subordination of private gain to public good. It means the investment of human and material resources in an imaginatively planned manner which can contribute to the vitality and progress of the nation, keep it in the mainstream of self-generating growth and development, raise the standard of living of the masses and bring forth the 'maximum gifts of each for the fullest enjoyment of all'.

∽

There is the other type of socialism which is socialism on the cheap, which feeds on slogans and promises, and thrives on the gullibility of the people.

This wrong brand of socialism is extremely

popular, because it is so much easier in practice. It mistakes 'Amiri hatao' for 'Garibi hatao'; it is content to satisfy the pangs of envy when it cannot satisfy the pangs of hunger; and, since it cannot create income or wealth, it plans for poverty and equal distribution of misery.

∽

The quintessence of socialism consists not in levelling down but in levelling up.

∽

Socialism and social justice are wholly different concepts. Socialism is to social justice what ritual is to religion and dogma to truth.

∽

State ownership and state control are the shells of socialism which were really intended to protect and promote the growth of the kernel, viz., social justice; but rigid shells merely constrict its growth.

∽

Social justice is often confused with mere equality. Social justice demands that there should be adequate differentials for ability and hard work, for education and expertise, for risk-bearing and willingness to take responsibility. Elimination of such differentials is the very negation of social justice.

❧

Socialism is like prohibition—it is a good idea but it doesn't work.

❧

While it is possible, in a poor country like India, to have economic growth without social justice, it is utterly impossible to have social justice without economic growth.

❧

'Distributive justice' can never get off to a start when there is nothing to distribute.

❧

Our brand of socialism did not result in transfer of wealth from the rich to the poor but only from the honest rich to the dishonest rich.

❧

The sleeping sickness of socialism is now universally acknowledged—but not officially in India.

Liberalization was to the 1990s what socialism was to the 1940s. Socialism is as outdated as the dinosaur. We now have insignificant ideologies; and our commanding heights have been reduced to molehills.

There is nothing like the unacceptable face of capitalism; in fact capitalism has no face of its own. It is the individual capitalist who has either an acceptable or unacceptable face depending on his conduct.

10

Union Budgets

Elections can change the governing faces; budgets can change the face of the state.

∽

Every budget contains a cartload of figures in black and white—but the stark figures represent the myriad lights and shades of India's life, the contrasting tones of poverty and wealth, and of bread so dear and flesh and blood so cheap, the deep tints of adventure and enterprise and man's ageless struggle for a brighter morn.

∽

The budget should not be an annual scourge but should partake of the presentation of annual accounts of a partnership between the government and the people. That partnership would work much better when the nonsensical secrecy is replaced by openness and public consultations, resulting in fair laws and the people's acceptance of their moral duty to pay.

∽

In India we have perfected the art of introducing budgets which aim at making all shades of political opinion unhappy and ensuring that they are made unhappy to the same extent.

∽

No budget can amend the laws of economics any more than it can the laws of dynamics.

∽

In trying to achieve the objective of levelling of income, our annual budgets merely succeed in widening the gulf between the dishonest rich and the poor, and narrowing the gap between the honest rich and the poor.

∽

India is the fabled land of contrasts, but there is no disparity so glaring and costly as that between the prized ends solemnly pronounced in the budget speech every year and the provisions of the annual Finance Bill which are so admirably calculated to frustrate those objectives.

❧

The biggest curse of the party system in any democracy is that it breeds a tendency to look at every measure on purely party lines. An almost universal tendency of all politicians is to view the budget not as a national budget but as a party budget. This causes either wholesale approval or total condemnation by those politicians whose critical perception is no higher than forty watts.

❧

Visionaries expect the finance minister to be the imaginative allocator of the nation's financial resources and the oracular orchestrator of the people's energies and enterprises, skills and disciplines. In practice, the minister is buffeted by the cross-currents of political pressures and by an unimaginable volume of contradictory advice proffered from all sides.

❧

Public ignorance is so colossal and our politicians'

knowledge of economics is so close to the freezing point that any incentive for industrial growth leads to the budget being branded as a 'rich man's budget'.

ॐ

A stable fiscal policy is to a nation what a stable family life is to an individual.

ॐ

Stability is anathema to the North Block. To preach the virtue of stability to our Finance Ministry is like seeking to preach the value of peaceful coexistence to Genghis Khan.

ॐ

1967-68: This year's budget has been described as a balanced budget—but it is balanced in the same way as is a tight-rope walker, which is not the best way for going very far.

ॐ

1970-71: The budget has been called an 'imaginative' budget. It is only so in the sense that it imagines certain consequences to ensue from the budget which are contrary to all known motivations of human nature and all rules of sound economics.

1971-72: The philosophy underlying the budget rests on the inarticulate major premises that (a) it is enough, and a lot easier, to impoverish the rich instead of enriching the poor; (b) the laws of human nature should be treated as impliedly and effectively repealed by the laws of Parliament; and (c) it is politically expedient to have a ceiling on income, although in practice it merely amounts to a ceiling on honesty.

∽

1974-75: To expect the budget to reverse the frightening trends (in poverty, unemployment, stagnation and inflation) is almost as reasonable as trimming a lawn with nail-scissors.

∽

1975-76: Like the budgets of several past years, this year's budget is again essentially a bullock-cart budget. A bullock-cart is an ancient and venerable vehicle, but not to be recommended for going places or reaching your destination expeditiously.

∽

1981-82: Four ingredients are to be found in any recipe for preparing a budget—psychology, politics, economics and strategy. The quality of the budget depends upon the quality of the ingredients and the proportion in which you mix them. This year's budget is psychologically perfect, politically clever, economically unsound and strategically a costly failure.

∽

1982-83: To a dehydrated nation, the budget offers water from an eye-dropper.

∽

1983-84: What was needed was a budget which would leave its mark on history. But we have been presented with a budget the effect of which will be as ephemeral as the scent on a pocket handkerchief.

∽

1985-86: The budget represents a silent and unheralded revolution in economic policy and fiscal thinking. The monumental task of redesigning India has begun.

It affords a refreshing contrast to the series of historically retrograde, economically unprogressive and socially stagnant budgets that preceded it in a supreme ironic procession for so many years.

∽

1986-87: If you are not confused by the budget, you are not well-informed!

⌘

1987-88: Those who had high hopes about the budget think that they would need a magnifying glass to find traces of relief in the finance bill.

⌘

1988-89: The finance minister has presented the country with a budget bouquet, made up of a few tiny fresh flowers at the front, and a lot of cheap greenery at the back sprayed with a soporific aroma—with some stinging nettles so well-concealed that they are not easily discernible to the superficial observer.

⌘

1989-90: Simplification is so wholly foreign to the culture of the Finance Ministry that perhaps the mistake was on the part of those who expected that quality in the budget.

⌘

1990-91: The budget which Mr Madhu Dandavate has introduced in Parliament is that of an honest humanist. It is not a budget to make you deliriously happy or to drive you to the verge of suicidal despair. It may be regarded as a good budget in bad times, though it might have ranked as a bad budget in good times.

☙

1992-93: Liberalization is the key to the budget. The only criticism can be that it measures out liberalization with coffee spoons.

☙

1993-94: On the whole, the budget is a harbinger of good times to come. It will not take India to heaven but it will check India's precipitate slide to hell.

☙

1994-95: The budget is historically important because it marks a turning point in the way Indians think about their economy—less like a tortoise and more like a tiger.

☙

II
Taxation

To tax and to please is not given to men; but to tax and be fair is.

∾

Taxes are the life-blood of any government, but it cannot be overlooked that that blood is taken from the arteries of the taxpayer and, therefore, the transfusion is not to be accomplished on dictates of political expediency but in accordance with the principles of justice and good conscience.

∾

Taxes, like water, have a tendency to find the lowest level. In the last analysis, almost all taxes ultimately hit the common man.

The rich pay *at* the high tax rates; but the entire nation pays *for* the high tax rates.

❧

Tax cuts are bound to prove economically efficient. No theory of socialism can get over the basic fact, hard as granite, that high rates of taxation inevitably result in the citizenry resorting to tax evasion. When the rates are vertiginous, the tax system breathes through the loopholes, and the economy breathes through the window of tax evasion. Over-taxation corrupts overtly.

❧

While death and taxes are inevitable, being taxed to death is not.

❧

The radiating potencies of taxes go far beyond mere raising of revenue. They propel tendencies which can obstruct effort, deflect enterprise and constrict growth.

❧

Any democratic government, which expects its people to rise and progress without incentives to work and save, has not the vaguest notion of the unalterable patterns of human nature and the eternal mainsprings of human action.

∽

Bad economics may temporarily be good politics; but politics should be kept behind a fiscal law, and not in front of it.

∽

Tax evasion is reprehensible: it is social injustice by the evader to his fellow citizens. Arbitrary or excessive taxation is equally reprehensible: it is social injustice by the government to the people.

∽

The days when the government could adopt any tax policy, as if the nation existed within a vacuum, are over.

∽

It is no doubt fair and in the national interest to check tax evasion with a firm hand; but it is neither fair nor in the national interest that the law should be made to bear hard on a large number of honest taxpayers merely in order to get at a few dishonest ones. To adapt a historic phrase, it is not right that so much should be inflicted on so many in order to rope in so few.

What is wrong with India is the pathological obsession displayed by the law-makers who frame laws only with the tax evader in mind, regardless of the enormous inconvenience and harassment to the far larger section of honest taxpayers.

In these matters one must have a balanced approach and a sense of proportion. A departmental store which is wholly preoccupied with prevention of shoplifting is a sure candidate for stagnation.

The Income-tax Act is a national disgrace. Yet more and more half-baked changes every few months are 'received calmly' by our people as part of their collective karma... Our laws are changed on the assumption that there is no intelligent life outside the North Block.

There is a growing tendency to enact arbitrary provisions which march with the hypotheses that the citizen exists for the state and not the state for the citizen, and that man is made for the law and not the law for man.

∽

When it is not necessary to change, it is necessary not to change.

∽

The tragedy of India is the tragedy of waste—waste of national time, energy and manpower. Tens of millions of man-hours, crammed with intelligence and knowledge—of taxgatherers, taxpayers and tax advisers—are squandered every year in grappling with the torrential spate of mindless amendments. The feverish activity achieves no more good than a fever.

∽

Precipitate and chronic tinkering with the law is fraught with insidious mischief. That all law is an experiment, as all life is an experiment, has been minted into the current coin of jurisprudence by Holmes. But experiments should not be so frequent, so short-sighted and so short-lived as to rob the law of that modicum of stability which is essential to its healthy growth.

The vagaries of the monsoon are less unpredictable than the whimsical changes in our tax laws.

The health of our economy will not improve until we inject the 'S' factor into our fiscal laws, and make them Sane, Simple and Stable.

Retrospective legislation is the bureaucrat's dream but the taxpayer's nightmare.

A perceptive scientist observed that insects have their own viewpoint about human civilization; a man thinks that he amounts to a great deal, but to a flea or a mosquito a human being is merely something good to eat. The attitude of the Finance Ministry towards our finest corporations is not much different.

A nation which will not let its industry retain sufficient funds to provide for obsolescence will itself soon become obsolescent.

On reduction of taxes at election time: Proverbial wisdom forbids you to look a gift horse in the mouth; but it does not forbid you to reflect whether the gift horse has been sent to you for keeps or has been merely lent to give you a single alluring ride to the ballot box.

On deletion of the statutory words requiring three years' notice to be given for abolishing investment allowance: The tax evader breaks the law. The government which abolished investment allowance without three years' notice equally broke the law. Does it make a difference that the government has the power to pass an amendment which is the fig leaf to cover up the flagrant breach of faith? Is there much to choose between a tax-evading citizen and a promise-evading government?

The fiscal system must have not merely legality but also legitimacy. It is denuded of all legitimacy when there are breaches of faith on the part of the government in its dealings with taxpayers.

The belief that the government will act on principles of honour and good faith is an invaluable but fragile national asset. The greatest mistake men in power make is to destroy that asset at their arrogant whim and fancy.

∽

When a government, which is so unfair and unjust, complains of tax evasion, it should remember that just as every nation gets the government it deserves, every government gets the taxpayers it deserves.

∽

Taxpayers' grievances remain unredressed for a very good reason. They do nothing more drastic than speak on the public platform, publish harmless booklets or write articles for newspapers which take up the space badly needed to publicize the latest homily and exhortation of some powerful individual in public office to the nation. They do not fast, nor do they set fire to themselves or to trams and buses. They do not lead morchas or processions to the Houses of Parliament. Above all, their number is relatively so small that any injustice to them, however strident, is of no political consequence whatsoever.

∽

If taxpayers were dogs, the officials of the Finance Ministry would undoubtedly be convicted under the Prevention of Cruelty to Animals Act.

∽

The time has come for Parliament to enact some new legislation—say, Prevention of Cruelty to Taxpayers Act—which should override all fiscal legislation.

∽

On denial of tax exemption to a charitable trust if its income is utilized for the benefit of the settlor or his relatives: It is a salutary principle of income-tax exemption that if you run a charity, you will not act on the principle that 'charity begins at home'.

∽

On an official of the Law Ministry expressing the view that the Nobel Prize of Mother Teresa might be liable to income-tax: The matter is so clear that the Finance Ministry should accept with grace the position that it is not entitled to any bite out of the moneys which are to go to the poorest of the poor. The law may be an ass, but it is not asinine enough to seek to tax a prize which is a token of humanity's gratitude to a saint. (*After this press statement, no attempt was made to tax Mother Teresa.*)

The proposal today (1994) is to levy service tax on three services... The proposed items chargeable to service tax will multiply as quickly as rabbits... Tax revenues are to Indian politicians what drugs are to junkies—they can never have enough. (*Service tax now covers all services—except a handful which are specifically excluded.*)

The expenditure tax (1957-1965) affected only a handful of citizens in this country, but a law which affects only a handful does not, on that account, justify its existence. A law which provides for the decapitation of all men over six feet will still be unfair, even if it affects only a very small minority of the nation.

12

Economics

To every economic policy and legislation we must apply the acid test—how far will it bend the talent, energy and time of our people to fruitful ends and how far will it dissipate them in coping with legal inanities and a bumbling bureaucracy.

∽

In the last analysis, economics is a matter of human nature and not a collection of nicely wrapped formulas ready to be applied to the ticklish and tangled problems which beset the country.

∽

You can either go forward or backward; you cannot stand still. This is a law of the universe, and it applies to economics as to every other human endeavour.

❦

In economics there are no miracles, there are only consequences—ruthless and inescapable consequences. The economic 'miracle' of Germany and of Japan is nothing but the predictable result of the fiscal vision of their government and discipline of their people.

❦

We keep on breezily tackling fifty-year problems with five-year plans, staffed by two-year officials, working with one-year appropriations, fondly hoping that somehow the laws of economics will be suspended because we are Indians.

❦

Development begins with people and not with goods.

❦

In our obsession with the Gross National Product, we have forgotten Gross National Happiness. Growth is concerned with the former, development with the latter. Growth is quantitative, development is qualitative. Quantitative growth counts, but qualitative development matters.

We do not want history to look upon our time as one in which pebbles were polished and diamonds were dimmed.

॰ঌ৹

The government can never create wealth, it can only spend it.

॰ঌ৹

Inflation is not self-correcting but self-accelerating; it rises with compound vengeance. Of all economic phenomena, it is the most ruthless, relentless and remorseless.

॰ঌ৹

On the government's counter-productive attempts to check inflation by effecting the credit squeeze, a freeze in wages and a cut in dividends: At best they merely amount to an attempt to cure the patient's fever by cooling the thermometer.

॰ঌ৹

Inflation is the invisible tax which has never been passed by Parliament.

॰ঌ৹

On employees' provident funds being compelled to invest in government securities yielding low interest: In other countries the government subsidizes the poor; in India the poor have to subsidize the government.

∽

World trade is a race in which India has to run in a potato sack, while other countries compete with no such handicap.

∽

On the reduction in fiscal deficit: The unborn generations are a group wholly unrepresented in Parliament, and to protect their vital interests it is essential that we bear the burden of our own debts.

∽

A nation's growth and prosperity depend upon the wise use of (a) tangible resources, (b) intangible resources like ability, energy and enterprise, and (c) time. The intangible resources and the time of the citizens are far more important than the tangible resources of the country. You can print money; you cannot print time. Time is more perishable than anything else; you cannot carry forward today's hours to tomorrow. No nation has a future where the administrative set-up ensures a tragic waste of the time and energy of the citizens.

❧

Collective progress is only the result of individual effort, and the government can achieve nothing without harnessing the boundless response, endeavour and enterprise of the citizens.

❧

It is a sad reflection on human nature, but a fact of life which we ignore only at our peril, that a man will work for himself and his family as he will work for no one else. Our laws fight a losing battle with the acquisitive instinct of man... Wise governments reasonably regulate these normal human instincts and ensure that they create open wealth for the nation. Foolish governments permit these instincts to create black markets and black money.

❧

I call it recession and the government calls it fall in demand. It is just like calling the mother, the father's wife.

❧

Earlier:

Most of our politicians and bureaucrats, untainted by knowledge of development in the outside world, have no desire to search for genes of ideas which deserve to be called 'a high-yielding variety of economics'. We are smugly reconciled, to quote Dr Sudhir Sen, to 'low yields from high ideals'.

∽

The sacred cows of economic theology (as distinct from economic rationalism) graze more plentifully in the North Block than in any other pasture.

∽

The method of eradicating economic inequalities by giddy levels of taxation involves levelling down. The modern fiscal method aims at levelling up and uses rapid economic growth as the one unfailing instrument for reduction of economic inequalities.

∽

Poverty is cruel, but it is curable. The only known cure is economic rationalism instead of economic theology. In the field of economics the tree of ideology has never borne any fruit.

∽

India is not poor by nature, but poor by policy. You would not be far wrong if you called India the world's leading expert in the art of perpetuating poverty.

☙

We were planning for scarcity instead of planning for abundance.

☙

The tide refused to roll back at the dictate of the King; and poverty has shown no signs of leaving India despite the stern and repeated admonition 'Garibi hatao' uttered by men in power.

☙

If we cannot have economic policies that make for plenty, let us at least have policies that make sense.

☙

Perhaps there is no other country on earth which has in such ample measure all the enterprise and skills needed to create national wealth, and which takes such deliberate and endless pains to restrict and hamper its creation.

☙

There is one way, and one way only, in which India can banish poverty, and that is by putting to the maximum productive use the 2000 million man-hours which fleet over India every day, never to come again.

∽

Surely something is basically wrong with our economic philosophy and political ideology if Indians are able to enrich foreign countries but are not allowed to solve the problem of poverty at home.

∽

It is the unshakable conviction of our government that the right thing to do economically is the wrong thing to do politically.

∽

No amount of slogan-mongering or munificent promises can get over the basic law of economics: you cannot divide more than you produce.

∽

The public sector does not necessarily mean public good and the private sector does not necessarily spell private gain. Our scarce financial resources should not be wasted on ideological preferences which envisage a dichotomy between the public sector and the private sector. The government and the people should think of only one sector—the national sector.

⚬

So far as the public sector is concerned, we are admonished to bear in mind the wise old rule, 'See no evil; hear no evil; speak no evil'. To believe or speak any evil of the public sector is merely to invite censure that you are not a patriot and not a true socialist.

⚬

Public sector enterprises are the black holes, the money guzzlers, and they have been extracting an exorbitant price for India's doctrinaire socialism.

⚬

History smiles when it sees a country seeking to reach the goal of a welfare state by a road which runs into lone and barren sands where honest enterprise is sorely tried and economic growth is held in chains.

⚬

We must refresh our jaded minds. Enterprise,

not control, makes production. Production, not legislation, makes prosperity.

∽

Brave words are used by various ministries suggesting the launching of a massive assault on inflation, stagnation, poverty and unemployment. After identifying the enemy, our first care should be to measure the enemy's strength and employ appropriate weapons. The experience of other countries shows the utility of sophisticated modern instruments which have ensured economic victory against heavy odds. But our Finance Ministry still believes in fighting only with bows and arrows.

∽

Later:

For the first forty years of our history as a republic, our leaders suffocated our people by state ownership and state control. During those lost decades the pace of our economic growth was sedate, if not glacial. Then came the economic transformation with a big bang. The period of collective insanity was over... The arthritic economy started performing like an athletic economy.

∽

In 1985 we began to change our course—silently and imperceptibly as a big ship does—from economic fundamentalism and sterile socialism to fruitful and meaningful egalitarianism.

∽

13
Politics

Bacon said, 'Knowledge is power'. A nation progresses gloriously when knowledge and power are combined in the same individuals. It faces a grave crisis when some have knowledge and others have power.

ॐ

The endeavour should be to reduce the IQ of our politicians. Do not think that it is a slip of the tongue on my part—IQ stands for Ignorance Quotient.

ॐ

Some minimum qualifications should be prescribed for those who seek election to Parliament... You need years of training to attend to a boiler or to mind a machine, to supervise a shop floor or to build a bridge, to argue a case in a law court or to operate upon a human body. But to steer the lives and destinies of millions of your fellowmen, you are not required to have any education or equipment at all!

∽

The overwhelming majority of our politicians are those of whom it may be said that their minds are some of the underdeveloped regions of the states they represent.

∽

Of some unthinking politicians, it can be truly said that if ignorance is bliss they ought to be the happiest men alive!

∽

The quality of our public life has reached its nadir. Politics has become tattered and tainted with crime... India today is a living example of the fact that cynicism corrupts and absolute cynicism corrupts absolutely.

∽

A commercial recession can be quickly transformed into a buoyant economy; but a moral recession cannot be shaken off for years. The rot in public life began after the death of Lal Bahadur Shastri and has been increasing at a galloping rate.

✑

Many of our politicians are unfit to lead the nation into anything except hot water. They have as much moral backbone as chocolate eclairs.

✑

We would as soon expect to find honesty and truthfulness in politicians as silence in a discotheque.

✑

The tone of public life has reached an all-time low. If the charges against various politicians in and out of power are to be investigated, India will need to have ombudsmen the way Australia has rabbits.

✑

Our Constitution aimed at making India the land of opportunity; our politicians have converted it into a land of opportunism.

✑

Nobody expects politics to be synonymous with ethics. But the unusual predicament facing India is that an